FRANCIS HENRY TAYLOR

PIERPONT MORGAN

AS COLLECTOR AND PATRON, 1837–1913

NEW YORK: THE PIERPONT MORGAN LIBRARY, 1970

The parallel so often drawn between Pierpont Morgan and Lorenzo de' Medici is one of the most accepted clichés of our generation. It is a dangerous generalization, for temperamentally they were as far apart as the poles. Yet each in his own way broke with his inherited tradition, and both men looked upon money as a source of maximum power and infallibility—never as an end in itself. And both induced in their contemporaries a new attitude towards the significance of works of art.

The year 1957 celebrated the Fiftieth Anniversary of the founding of the Pierpont Morgan Library—five decades of glorious and unprecedented service to scholarship and beauty in this country. But few who are alive today—even among those whose memories reach back to its early beginnings—realize that the Library had its roots as much as a century ago in the formative years from 1854 to 1857 when Pierpont Morgan, first as a schoolboy in Switzerland and then as an affiliate of a student corps at the University of Göttingen, laid the foundations of his tastes and appetites by frugally acquiring from his limited pocket money objects of art which had caught his as yet untutored eye.

When the young Morgan returned to America to enter business in the autumn of 1857, the country was on the threshold of a renaissance. The break with the Royal Academy which, because of Benjamin West's Philadelphian origin, was so close to the hearts of our artists of the eighteenth century, had already taken place. A group of expatriates, painters, and marble cutters had extended themselves from Rome to Düsseldorf and Munich; Paris had not yet become the Mecca that it was to be in the '80's and '90's. A consciousness of the New World was stirring and "manifest destiny," if it was not yet on the lips of the *literati,* was nonetheless uppermost in their minds. Collecting was of the most modest order—a pale shadow of the gentleman's curio cabinet in England and on the Continent. The elevation of the intellect was measured by the exaltation of the soul. It was, however, a sternly Protestant vision which was revealed. Man, it was conceded, could not live by bread alone but it was only the wholesome whole-wheat loaf that could suffer to have spread upon it the locusts and wild honey of humanism. Both Lorenzo and the new Magnifico had his own John the Baptist; the difference between them being that whereas the appearance of the former had been foretold by Dante a century before, Pierpont Morgan was heralded only by William Cullen Bryant crying in the wilderness.

Lorenzo's grandfather, Cosimo, was a self-made man and despot who had consolidated his leadership of Florence through forced loans and punitive taxation, weapons which he managed as deftly as others used the dagger. Pierpont Morgan on the other hand was descended from five generations of Morgans who had owned and farmed their land in the Connecticut River valley from 1638 to 1817, and his mother's family had produced respected merchants, farmers and theologians for a hundred and fifty years. The Europeans who have tried to explain the Morgan passion for luxury and collecting in terms of their own experience—that is to say in the light of the tastes and activities of the new *haute bourgeoisie* of the post-Napoleonic Industrial Revolution—have never understood, nor made any effort to understand, the background of his upbringing. Only in England, where the great commoner families of the landed gentry had always occupied a far more influential position than the *noblesse de la robe,* was there any real insight into Pierpont Morgan's character and motives. And it is unquestionably this mutuality of sympathy which so attracted him to London.

Unlike other captains of American industry who adorned their success with the emblems of a past glory in order to buy a measure of security in the closing years of this life and a doubtful immortality in the next, Pierpont Morgan enjoyed the pleasures of the present for their own sake, knowing full well that in the hands of his Redeemer a final accounting would take place. In this respect he was always Church and never Chapel. Uncompromising and self-indulgent though he may have been, he accepted both material and spiritual gratification in the spirit of a *grand seigneur*. He never whined nor concealed his motives with the tight-lipped phrases of the Covenanter. He received the German Emperor aboard the *Corsair* in the same spirit with which he attended the private luncheon at Windsor following the funeral of Edward VII or shared a familiar and easy intimacy at Lambeth with the Archbishop of Canterbury. He was almost the first American, ironically enough, since Benjamin Franklin and Thomas Jefferson—and perhaps the last—who dared to be a gentleman of the world without setting up a foundation to accomplish his purpose and without a board of trustees to bolster his inferiority. Although he disposed of a fortune estimated at upwards of $100,000,000—and this was before the inducements of the Income Tax—giving lavishly to the causes in which he believed, and providing at his death in 1913 for many princely benefactions, the word "philanthropy" does not seem to have existed in his vocabulary. And in the many bound volumes of press clippings preserved in the Morgan Library the writers of his obituaries also seem, consciously or unconsciously, not to have used the term. Perhaps they were too dazzled by the magnificence, the power and the vitality of the man himself.

So simple and direct and yet so complex a personality must have manifested itself quite early in Pierpont Morgan's career. As so often is the case with great historic figures, the salient features of his character had, in fact, revealed themselves by his fifteenth birthday, for circumstances as well as the fashion of his day had forced him to take responsibilities and to make decisions which today seldom confront the American schoolboy. In the comparative solitude of the Azores and Europe and separation from his friends and family in Hartford and Boston, he developed the pattern of long silences and resolute reliance upon his personal opinions and decisions which brought such terror to the unwary in his later life. Throughout the many years of his almost volcanic activity the basic emotional conflict between his homespun Yankee background and sophisticated continental schooling is constantly breaking the surface.

The modest foundation of the Morgan fortune had been laid by generations of farmers culminating in Pierpont's grandfather, Joseph Morgan, Jr., a captain in General Washington's army and a responsible citizen of West Springfield. His son, Joseph III, moved to Hartford, where he became a hotel owner and was one of the founders of the Aetna Fire Insurance Company. He was also engaged in several transportation enterprises: a steamboat line, a canal company, and the new railroad from Hartford to Springfield. His son, Junius Spencer Morgan, the father of Pierpont, entered the dry goods business in Hartford at the age of 23, remaining there until 1851, when he transferred to Boston as a partner in J. M. Beebe, Morgan & Company, a firm that conducted and financed foreign trade transactions, especially in cotton. In 1854, George Peabody of Salem, who was already established as one of the most prosperous merchant–bankers in London, and was looking for an American partner to succeed him, persuaded Junius Morgan to transplant himself to England. During our Civil War Peabody retired, and the firm, which had achieved a commanding position in the sale of American securities in England, took the name of J. S. Morgan & Co.

Frank Harris in *Latest Contemporary Portraits* (New York, 1927) has left us a rather sympathetic glimpse of Junius Morgan. He was "observant rather than intuitive and articulate"—"an excellent listener"—and the style of his living was "everything comfortable,

[6]

nothing ostentatious." They were on pleasant terms as neighbors on the Riviera and after Junius Morgan's death at Èze in a carriage accident in April 1890 Harris observed, "I was surprised when I read in the paper that he had left some £2,600,000 to his son Pierpont Morgan. He lived as an English gentleman would live who was making forty or fifty thousand a year. . . He had all the reticences of the Anglo-Saxon, and probably unbosomed himself but seldom, even to his intimates."

While the family was still living in Boston, young Pierpont was struck down with what today might possibly be diagnosed as a mild attack of polio but which in those days passed for inflammatory rheumatism. His health was depleted and when he recovered, one of his legs was shorter than the other. A warmer climate and a period of rest from his studies was prescribed and the young boy of fifteen was shipped off in November 1852 on the barque *Io* to the island of Fayal in the Azores. Although strictly on his own, living modestly in a primitive hotel, he was under the fatherly supervision of the American consul, Charles W. Dabney, whose family, long-time residents at Horta, had been friends of the Morgans.

The faithful and prolific letters Pierpont wrote home show already his incipient interest in international finance and in making his limited allowance for living expenses and pocket money go as far as possible, surviving even the intricacies of foreign exchange. He lived close to the Portuguese fisherfolk and in the long periods of his ocean crossings he developed that passion for maritime life and yachting which was to last throughout his life. The letters also are filled with minute descriptions of the trinkets and souvenirs which he sent home as presents to his family and friends, descriptions which reveal the intensity of his observation and his love of craftsmanship for its own sake. Possibly here is the beginning of his predilection for the decorative arts which made him accumulate them later in such profusion.

[7]

Neither his eye nor his taste was yet in any way developed, but already one senses his acquisitive instinct for the three-dimensional object and the article of personal and especially of historic association. Although in later life he surrounded himself with great masterpieces of painting he was always more interested in the artifact than in the image. As *The Burlington Magazine* observed editorially after his death, "his feeling for works of art was the outcome rather of a romantic and historical feeling for the splendor of past ages than a strictly aesthetic one. What he recognized in an object was primarily its importance, the part it had played in the evolution of civilization."

His health was completely recovered and he left Horta in April 1853 on the steamship *Great Western* for Southampton to join his parents. In the week which he spent alone in London he visited Buckingham Palace, the House of Lords, Westminster Abbey, Madame Tussaud's Waxworks and the Bank of England. What sixteen-year-old American would do this today without prompting? In Manchester, Pierpont met his parents who had arrived from America, and he and his mother drove to Stratford, then on to Warwick Castle and Oxford. Returning to London he amused himself at Albert Smith's panorama of the "Ascent of Mont Blanc," the popular circus known as "Astley's Amphitheatre," the horticultural exhibition at Chiswick, and "The Wellington Campaigns." He also inspected the Tower, the tunnel under the Thames, and St. Paul's, "climbing up to the very summit into the ball." The culmination of this London experience was described in the laconic words, "Went into the City and to Mr. Camroux who took us over the Bank of England, and I held 1,000,000 pounds in my hands."

On the 20th of May 1853 young Pierpont began with his family the first of those European Grand Tours which were to play such an important role in the development of his appetites and inclinations. First Brussels, via Dover and Calais, then Cologne and on to Berlin, where at an exhibition he had his first glimpse of royalty in the person of the King of Prussia and his family. The experience was repeated at Sunday Church services in Dresden, where he saw the King of Saxony and his family and spent the afternoon at the picture gallery. The travelers visited Leipzig and Cologne, taking the Rhine steamer from Bonn to Coblenz, then going on to Cassel and Frankfort. From Baden-Baden and Strassburg they traveled by slow degrees to Paris, where they stayed at the Hôtel de Lille et d'Albion in the rue Saint-Honoré. Among other diversions Pierpont went to the Opera and the Hippodrome, where he saw Napoleon III and the Empress Eugénie.

Paris on this occasion did not make much of an impression upon him—in fact, although he spoke French fluently and was there many times, he never seems to have referred to the city with the pleasure or affection that he always showed towards London and Rome. After this hurried visit, largely for his mother's shopping, they returned to England for a brief tour of Northern England, Scotland, Ireland and Wales before sailing at the end of July for America.

But even in these hectic weeks of travel the young tourist saw much that was to mold his innate sense of the past—Glasgow, the Trossachs, Loch Lomond and Loch Katrine, names which were to reappear in the literary manuscripts of the Library. He visited Holyrood Palace and Edinburgh Castle, Abbotsford, Melrose Abbey, Ripon and Fountains Abbey. The party went on to York and Sheffield, driving over to spend the day at the Duke of Devonshire's noble house of Chatsworth. Paxton was in his zenith; the great works for the visit of the Queen had been completed and Chatsworth was one of the famous sights of England. Yet it was the house itself which must have commanded his attention. One wonders also whether it was not his introduction to the Duke of Devonshire's incomparable library which sowed the seed for its counterpart on Thirty-sixth Street.

An uneventful journey from Liverpool via Halifax brought the young Morgan back to Boston for his final exposure to American education at the English High School. Although he had missed a year he continued with his graduating class. There must have been some of the inevitable sententiousness of the much-traveled young man, for in writing to his cousin and best friend, Jim Goodwin, about a book he had sent him, he could not resist adding, "That seal I used was a copy of Mary Queen of Scots' signet ring which I procured at Holyrood Palace, Edinburgh. M. R. is Mary Regina." How he must have relished his success when as an old man he was able to assemble an important collection of documentary material relating to the Queen, including a fourteen-page autograph letter from Mary to her uncle, the Duc de Guise.

The final year in Boston was merely a preparation for the next three years abroad. The family moved to London in the autumn of 1854 and it was arranged for Pierpont to enter the Institut Sillig at "Bellerive" in the outskirts of Vevey on the Lake of Geneva. He was not a pensionnaire but had rooms in a chalet close by. His record there was undistinguished except in mathematics; he managed to be both gay and industrious. He was liked by Monsieur and Madame Sillig and popular particularly with the American boys, Charles and Frank Payson, Cassius Gilmore, James Wadsworth, William G. Tiffany, Gerard Beekman and William Riggs. These were friendships which were destined to last throughout their lives and the New York dinners of the "Sillig boys" were frequently recurring events. During this period the young Morgan quickly grew to manhood in the manner of European youth, and it was probably at the Institut Sillig that he acquired his first knowledge of and enthusiasm for art. His inseparable companion, William Riggs, in later life preceded Morgan as an officer of the Metropolitan, and in 1913 the Museum received the gift of Riggs's pre-eminent collection of armor and art.

There is in the possession of the Morgan Library an account book of Pierpont Morgan for 1854 to 1857 listing all money received from home. It is complete down to the least detail and is a rather touching document, for it contains records of pocket money, illnesses, gifts to beggars, what he spent on cuff links and school books, what he paid for every meal outside of school, and incidental expenses such as 2 francs for ice creams, 2 francs for cravats, and 28 francs for shirts. He was already in the habit of giving lavish presents to his friends and he also spent 20 centimes for a visit to a salt mine, and 4 fr. 50 for "panes of glass broken." He formed a habit of buying post-cards and views of the sights which he visited.

In the summer of 1855 he visited the great Exposition of Napoleon III, and twice attended the Beaux-Arts Exhibition, held in a separate pavilion on the site of the present Grand Palais; here he bought a catalogue for 2 francs, and he did the same during a visit to Versailles. He entered 50 centimes for checking parasols at the Gobelin tapestry works and only 30 centimes for the same purpose at the Louvre.

In April 1856 he enrolled at the University of Göttingen, and there his tastes became increasingly adult. We find him giving more money to charities and spending more on books and "refreshments." He also made many side trips to Münden and Cassel, and visited Frankfort and Wiesbaden. He was apparently an alert if not profound student of history and did so well in mathematics that his professor begged him to remain in order to qualify for a university chair in that field. His French and German stayed with him all his life and the marginal comments which he made on his later Italian correspondence show that he read that language easily. His amusements were "academical concerts" and dancing lessons. Already he had developed a taste for fancy pipes and Havana cigars, and his expenditures for tobacco were out of all proportion to his very simple scale of living.

The next six months after leaving Göttingen in January 1857 were devoted to resuming the Grand Tour and to the further preparation of Pierpont Morgan the collector. He went first to Paris and thence by train, *diligence* and sailing vessels, via Lyons, Marseilles, Hyères and Toulon, to Rome. Still only 19, he spent several months alone visiting the proper sights in Italy, and was inspired by the achievements of the Italian Renaissance. During seven weeks in Rome he made his first purchases of works of art, which cost him two and a half times as much as the total of his living expenses for this sojourn. His purchases included a mosaic picture of the *Tomb of Caecilia Metella,* a copy of Guido Reni's *Hope,* an Etruscan brooch, reproductions of a Canova *Hebe, The Dying Gladiator,* and *The Dogs of the Capitol,* and "a vase of oriental alabaster." Contemporary art was represented by busts of a *Madonna* and an *Angel of the Annunciation* by Benzoni, whose work in the Piazza di Spagna had probably caught Pierpont's fancy as he came and went from his lodgings there.

At Naples he purchased an expensive coral necklace for his sister Sarah, and a lava ink stand. By the time he reached Florence his money may have been running low, but he nevertheless acquired for his collection a box in wooden mosaic and a mosaic paper weight. Among the sights he visited were the Corsini Palace, "Michelangelo's house," Santa Maria Novella, San Miniato, and "Galileo's town" (Arcetri). Fifty years later he may have smiled when he was offered the Strozzi Palace for 3,000,000 francs—and turned it down.

After this brief preliminary skirmish with the money-changers in the temples of the Muse, Pierpont Morgan, now a man of the world of twenty years, was almost ready to set his face towards home and a business career. His cousin Jim Goodwin joined him for a final short tour of Belgium, Germany, and Austria, during which he revisited Göttingen to wind up his affairs and give a farewell party which included champagne. In July he returned to London to take leave of his family before starting for America.

Expenses Rome April 1857

Expenses landing at Civita Vecchia	37
Custom House Expenses	70
Passport Expenses at Civita Vecchia	1 30
Breakfast	60
Diligence fare to Rome	1 86
Porters, Postillons & Conductors	95
Breakfast Apl 11th	40
St Johns Lateran	20
1/2 Carriage for Civita Vecchia	9 30
Lodging two nights	5 "
Porterage 40 Carriage 20	60
Carriage 28	28
Expenses of Passport	65
Bronze vases — Pompeii —	12 "
Bronze lamp & marble vase	39 "
Lunch	10 "
Wine 80 Packing 50	1 30
Loss on Specie 25 Scudi	37
Amount Carried for'd Scudi	74 98

Amount brot for'd Scudi	74 98
Washing	59
Dr Bill	4 —
Passport Expenses	25
Packing box	20
Inspector of the fine arts	1 50
Polishing marbles	40
Dinners for the week	2 30
Supplement Diligence to Vecchia	3 10
Loss on Specie	26
Carriage to Vatican	35
Copy of Canova's Hebe	—
Copy of Dying Gladiator	—
The Dogs of the Capitol	—
Vase of Oriental Alabaster	235 50
Busts of the Madonna & Angel	
of Annunciation by Benzoni	170 —
Copy by Akers of Young Augustus	41 "
Packing bill at Boschetti	6 80
Porterage	40
Amt carried over Scudi	541 63

Cash Account Book kept by Pierpont Morgan.

London in the summer of 1857 must have been an exciting place for a young man. The Crimean War was over but the marching songs of Empire were stirring everywhere. Prince Albert, flushed with the success of the Great Exhibition of 1851, was busy humanizing the British and imposing a Germanic sense of order upon the artists and patrons of his adopted country. The Crystal Palace had been rebuilt at Sydenham and we know that Pierpont Morgan went there at least twice. From it he gained an even better insight into the relation of the arts and industry than he had at the Beaux-Arts Exhibition in Paris two years previously. With his peculiar turn of mind it must have had a profound effect upon him. Although he sailed from Liverpool late in July it is curious that he did not stop off in Manchester to see the great Exhibition of Art Treasures—the greatest exhibition of works of art from private collections ever held in the nineteenth century.

But the young Morgan was impatient to return to the New World. His education was behind him and he was eager to try his fortune in the market place. Years must elapse before he could indulge once again in the delights he had tasted abroad. He seems to have shut himself off from them quite deliberately in order to apply himself the more rigorously to the world of finance. He began as an unsalaried junior accountant in a New York firm of private bankers, Duncan, Sherman & Co. It was not altogether a happy association for there seemed to be a tendency at first to underestimate this self-confident and taciturn European-trained youth and to consider him merely a *fils à Papa*. After four years of uneasy apprenticeship, he determined to have his own firm, and ultimately persuaded his colleague at Duncan, Sherman, C. H. Dabney, to join him in forming Dabney, Morgan & Co. This new partnership was strengthened by becoming the American agent of the senior Morgan's London firm. Upon Dabney's retirement in 1871, Pierpont, who was over-tired and suffered from recurrent fainting spells, thought seriously of giving up business, but an urgent offer from Anthony J. Drexel of Philadelphia persuaded him to continue as a Drexel partner. In July, 1871, the historic firm of Drexel, Morgan & Co. opened its books.

It was a frenzied moment in American history. The Civil War was concluded and "Reconstruction" had set in. The state governments in many parts of the country had repudiated their debts and the large refunding operations of the federal government were taking place. The railroad wars were also at their height and the English investors were deeply involved. It was at this point that the Morgans, father and son, stepped into the fray. "By their courage, determination and integrity they were responsible," in the words of Samuel J. Tilden, for "upholding unsullied the honor of America in the tabernacle of the Old World." From then on the House of Morgan became, in the closing years of the nineteenth century and the first decades of the twentieth, both the symbol of and the spokesman for a new code of ethics in American business. From this peculiar circumstance Pierpont Morgan derived a personal and moral prestige which extended far beyond the material evidences of his private fortune.

His earliest years in business were beclouded for Morgan by the death, four months after their marriage, of his first wife Amelia Sturges. Three years later he married Frances Louisa Tracy and during the '60's and '70's they lived quietly and simply in a succession of houses in Manhattan's Murray Hill neighborhood, finally establishing themselves in 1882 at 219 Madison Avenue, on the corner of 36th Street. According to legend Pierpont Morgan's first purchase of a work of art was an oil painting of "a young and delicate woman by an artist named Baker and the price was $1,500." It was said that he bought this painting in 1864 at the Sanitary Commission Fair—a bazaar for the benefit of the sick and wounded in the Civil War (the Commission would roughly correspond to today's Red Cross). The legend was further embellished by the suggestion that the portrait reminded him of his first wife "Mimi" Sturges. But the picture is signed and dated 1874, ten years after the Fair took place. Although a photograph of the drawing room of the New York house occupied by the Morgans in the '70's shows a number of paintings crowding the walls, no significant art purchases appear to be recorded until the middle '80's. And a catalogue of Morgan's books, printed in 1883, reveals little more than a good reading library, containing a number of useful art books, sets of standard authors, and a sprinkling of rare autographs.

The New York town houses at this early date were for the most part relatively modest. The individual grandeur and spaciousness of the residences which had a generation earlier graced Washington Square and Gramercy Park had given way to a uniform brownstone façade. They were as smug as they were comfortable; from the point of view of architecture they were utterly without distinction. They epitomized a life of bourgeois luxury which welcomed neither new ideas nor new faces. It was an enclave on the tight little Island of Manhattan peopled with the characters from Mrs. Edith Wharton's novels. Society was conservative, somewhat timid, and deeply impressed with any contact with the aristocracy of Europe. Nevertheless some of the newer millionaires were moving uptown to a Fifth Avenue magnificence which permitted Murray Hill to glory in its general air of stuffiness.

The great dynastic fortunes were still relatively few. So far as the arts were concerned, it was not yet necessary to conjure with such names as Carnegie, Frick and Rockefeller. The Astors at no time have shown a predilection for art and the Whitneys and the Vanderbilts, with the exception of William K., were comparatively late-comers on the scene. Among Philadelphian connoisseurs, the names of Drexel and Widener were just beginning to be recognized.

Murray Hill was a law unto itself—a pleasant residential village in which old New Yorkers of the Dutch and English families of the eighteenth century had admitted the more prosperous and cultivated business families to their inner circle. If one reads the lists of the governing bodies and incorporators of the great New York institutions—the New-York Historical Society, the American Museum of Natural History, and the Metropolitan Museum—in the middle decades of the century—say from 1830 to 1870—it appears that the solid if unspectacular wealth was largely derived from the increase in real estate values as the port of New York climbed to world importance. The moneys realized in this way were either reinvested in Manhattan or used speculatively in the opening of the West. There was little margin left during the second half of the century for the collecting of art in the sense that it was being done abroad or even with the modest discrimination known in this country between the War of 1812 and the Panic of 1837, when it seemed possible for a brief moment that collecting might become a major American preoccupation.

There were of course a few notable exceptions to this rule. Tuckerman's *Book of the Artists* listed in 1867 the following collections in New York City: August Belmont, W. H. Aspinwall, A. T. Stewart, W. T. Blodgett, Cyrus Butler, A. M. Cozzens, Robert Hoe, John Taylor Johnston, James Lenox, R. M. Olyphant, Marshall O. Roberts, R. L. Stuart, and Jonathan Sturges. Virtually nothing in these cabinets except the rare books and manuscripts belonging to Hoe and Lenox would be looked at twice today by the curators or purchasing committees of any of the New York museums. The New-York Historical Society had more by good luck than good management stumbled into some rather fine antiquities and a certain group of interesting and genuine, but not superlative, primitives that had once formed the nucleus of Bryan's Gallery of Christian Art. They had deliberately brushed away an opportunity of acquiring the

Pierpont Morgan about 1861.

Jarves primitives now at Yale, and New York had by default allowed Boston and Philadelphia to continue as the cultural centers of the country.

One man alone made up for the deficiency of these lean artistic years, Henry G. Marquand, one of the founders of the Metropolitan Museum and its second president. Measured by any standards in Europe and in almost any age he was a great connoisseur. The group of 35 paintings which he gave to the Metropolitan in 1883 still ranks among its proudest possessions: the Rembrandt and Van Dyck portraits, the Vermeer *Young Woman at a Casement,* and a half dozen other treasures are comparable to the pictures which Lord Hertford and Sir Richard Wallace were pouring into Manchester Square. Marquand is one of the nearly forgotten and unsung heroes of American collecting, but his achievements stand out in splendid isolation from those of his successors in the extravagant Age of Duveen.

It was into this quiet milieu that Pierpont Morgan slipped almost anonymously in the years of his intense financial activity. Always self-confident, with a sense of responsibility to great causes—such as the trusteeships of the Metropolitan and the American Museum of Natural History, and his lifelong devotion to St. George's Church and the problems of the Protestant Episcopal Church in America—he lived elegantly but without ostentation, much in the manner of an English heir, not wishing in any way to appear to anticipate the titles and estates which would naturally befall him. His reluctance to start the art collecting which had been in his mind since his university days at Göttingen was not so much because of the comparatively limited resources at his command—for he was already a wealthy man—but rather out of a deep sense of primogeniture and filial respect. If any Morgan was going to collect it was the privilege of the father to do so, not the son. That Pierpont Morgan withheld his thunderbolts for more than thirty years after his return from Europe

[17]

made the reverberations of the last twenty years of his life in the art world, when he finally unleashed them, the louder and the more electric.

Morgan's most recent, and in fact his best, biographer, Frederick Lewis Allen, said of him that he "was by nature a duke of industry, pursuing the life of an unostentatious gentleman on a majestic scale." This is perhaps the quality that marked the years following his inheritance, which by virtue of the very paradox implicit in the phrase made him so little understood and subject to such virulent and undeserved vituperation. Since he was intimate with few persons in either the business or the art world he became a legend, an easy synonym for some mysterious and corporate gluttony. No one was willing to concede that a collector who bought so much could possibly know what he was buying. For every art dealer who was lucky enough to sell to him there were a hundred who must find consolation for their failures. The easiest way to save face and heal one's wounded pride was to accuse Morgan of being a vulgar wholesaler, a man who depended solely on other people's eyes and judgment and who was himself lacking in that rarefied and indefinable thing called taste. For art serves always as a form of defense mechanism for both the owner and the vendor.

It is not so much that the grass is greener in the other fellow's yard as it is that the grapes in Naboth's vineyard too easily turn to vinegar. What in their bitterness Morgan's critics failed to recollect was that he was primarily a cultivated man of the world with a much better European education than the average antiquary possessed, and that he was sufficiently at home both in England and on the Continent not to be taken in by the trade. It was characteristic of him that he was almost never impressed by the outward trappings of any man. He relied not upon the fairy stories the dealers told him nor upon certificates of experts, but upon his private estimate of their character and integrity.

Although the Morgan Library is filled with letters and documents relating to the acquisitions made during Pierpont Morgan's lifetime and by his son, there is little in the way of guidance through the complicated history of the collections. The handwritten "chronology" prepared by Herbert L. Satterlee when he was working on the *Life* of his father-in-law is more useful in many ways than the book itself. Two excellent summaries of the collections appeared in *The Times* of London, one published December 4, 1908, dealing exclusively with the Library, the other an obituary memoir published April 1, 1913. Both of these excellent pieces are unsigned but are certainly the work of knowledgeable and sympathetic writers. Bishop William Lawrence of Massachusetts, who was frequently Morgan's guest in America and abroad, has left us a most vivid informal account of the London house at Prince's Gate, which, together with an English country place, Dover House, Morgan had inherited from his father. Bishop Lawrence's sympathetic picture of the character of his friend is penetrating and realistic. Finally there is the schedule of Morgan gifts appended to the resolution of the Trustees of the Metropolitan Museum of Art and published in the *Bulletin* for January 1918. To these sources, to the article by George K. Boyce on the Library in *The Library Quarterly* (January, 1952), and to the encyclopedic and patient investigations of Miss Mary M. Kenway in the Library's archives, the present account of the collections formed between 1890 and Morgan's death in 1913 owes its existence.

At the very outset Pierpont Morgan found it to his advantage to lean upon those whom he could trust. Among the first of these was his nephew, Junius S. Morgan, a man of slenderer means but a passionate connoisseur of books, prints and engravings, and literary properties of all sorts. Also to his nephew he owed the discovery of a young assistant in the Princeton University Library, Miss Belle da Costa Greene, who became his librarian and confidential art secretary in 1905 and was later the first Director of the Library. Until her death in 1950, she was one of the greatest figures in the art and bibliophile worlds, a person to whom American scholarship in general and the Library in particular must always be indebted.

By the middle '90's Morgan's collecting of individual items for the Library was in full swing; they ranged from the Gutenberg Bible on vellum to the original manuscript of Keats's *Endymion*. In 1899 Morgan made his first *en bloc* purchase: the late James Toovey's "library of leather and literature," including a remarkable run of Aldines, and a fine series of tooled leather bindings. The following year he purchased the best part of the library of Theodore Irwin of Oswego, New York, which included the Duke of Hamilton's famous "Golden Gospels" and a manuscript Apocalypse that had belonged to the duc de Berry. But the biggest *coup* of all was the purchase in 1902 of the collection of Richard Bennett of Manchester, of which the core was the library of William Morris. Bennett's collection consisted of about 700 volumes, carefully selected for significance and rarity, including more than a hundred illuminated manuscripts. Among the incunabula were 32 Caxtons, and in this respect the Bennett Collection ranked the fourth largest in existence. The Collection was purchased by Morgan at a price said to be about $700,000, and was the largest single purchase ever made for the Library. After the completion of his new library building in 1906, Morgan made only two large group purchases: the Wakeman Collection of American literary MSS in 1909, and the Fairfax Murray Collection of drawings in 1910. The rest of his abundant purchases were made individually or in small groups.

(*Above*) The Library at 219 Madison Avenue, about 1890.
(*Below*) The West Room of the Pierpont Morgan Library, about 1910.

But let us turn for a moment from the acquisitions for the Library to the works of art which filled the house at Prince's Gate. There we see the very heart of the matter, collections which were not gathered up in the onrushing tide of his major design but were instead the items which he selected piece by piece and with which he chose to live. No journalist was ever permitted to invade its privacy, so Bishop Lawrence's keen and faithful observations are doubly precious. It is the only description of the Morgan residence by an eye witness that exists:

I doubt whether there has ever been a private dwelling house so filled with works of the richest art. As one entered the front door, he was still in a conventional London house, until passing along three or four yards, his eye turned and looked through the door on the left into the dining-room—in size an ample city dining-room, but in glory of color such as few other domestic dining-rooms ever enjoyed. The visitor was amazed and thrilled at the pictures: Sir Joshua Reynolds' masterpiece, *Madame Delmé and Children*, a great full-length portrait of a lady by Gainsborough, another [of *Mrs. Scott-Jackson*] by Romney. One's eye seemed to pierce the wall into the outer world through the landscapes of Constable [*The White Horse*] and Hobbema. Behind Mr. Morgan's chair at the end of the table hung a lovely Hoppner of three children [*The Goodsall Children*], a beautiful boy standing in the center, full of grace. Why did Mr. Morgan have this picture behind him? If you would sit in his chair, which faced the front of the house with the two windows looking out upon the hedge and trees of Hyde Park, you would discover between these two windows a narrow mirror, which enabled Mr. Morgan to have before him always the reflected portrait of the figure of the boy. As one passed through the hall, each picture was a gem. In the center of the hall, where the dividing wall used to stand, was a graceful bronze figure, turning at will upon its base, once the weather vane of the Sainte Chapelle [*Ange de Lude* now in the Frick collection]; near it a stone figure from the Duomo of Florence; cabinets standing about with reliquaries, statuettes and other figures.

Before going into the two rooms at the back, one passed upstairs to the next floor and entered a large drawing-room at the left. The beautiful *Elizabeth [Georgiana], Duchess of Devonshire,* by Gainsborough, looked down from the mantel. When I saw it for the first time, my memory slipped back [to Mr. Morgan's story of] how he gained possession of the picture. It was, as everybody knows, stolen in 1876 immediately after it had been purchased by Messrs. Agnew at the Wynn-Ellis sale at a large price. At the end of twenty-five years it was discovered in Chicago, and in April 1901, was given back to Messrs. Agnew. Mr. Morgan said that one day in 1901, after a short absence from New York, as he came home his butler said that a representative of the Messrs. Agnew had called and that he had the *Duchess of Devonshire* with him. "Where is he?" asked Mr. Morgan, "I want to see him." "He was just going to sail for home and is gone." Mr. Morgan said, "I was determined to have that picture and I took the next ship for England. My ship was faster than his. He arrived in London on Saturday, I on Sunday. I sent word to one of the firm that I must see him on Monday morning before he went down town. He came to Prince's Gate, and I said, "You have the *Duchess of Devonshire*." "Yes," he replied. "You remember that my father on the afternoon before that picture was stolen was about to buy it and was going to make his decision the next morning. He wanted it. What my father wanted, I want, and I must have the *Duchess*." "Very good," said the dealer. "What is the price?" asked Mr. Morgan. "That is for you to say, Mr. Morgan." "No, whatever price your firm thinks is fair, I pay." And the *Duchess of Devonshire* . . . was hung in Prince's Gate.

Turning from her, one's eye glanced about the room and recognized portraits made familiar through prints and engravings of a Rembrandt, a Frans Hals, a child by Velasquez, and the magnificent Van Dyck *Woman in Red and Child*. Two or three tables solid, with shallow drawers, stood in the room. As we opened one drawer after another, the wealth of beauty, color and fineness of execution of hundreds of miniatures were disclosed. As we took up one miniature after another, small and large, we realized not only the beauty of the miniature but the wealth and appropriateness of the frame, for when a miniature had been purchased with an unworthy frame, an artist had designed a frame in harmony with the style of the date of the miniature and set it round with gold and often with rows of pearls and diamonds. Each miniature with its frame seemed to compose one beautiful cluster of jewels.

These miniatures, for which Dr. Williamson wrote the *de luxe* catalogue, comprised one of the most celebrated cabinets ever formed. They have since been dispersed by private treaty and at public auction. The English series ranged from the time of Holbein to Queen Victoria. By Holbein there were miniatures of Henry VIII (painted as a royal gift for Anne of Cleves), of Sir Thomas More (now in the Metropolitan), and of Nicholas Kratzer, the astronomer, whose portrait by the same hand is in the Louvre. Hilliard was represented by a miniature of the young Princess, afterwards Queen, Elizabeth; three of the beautiful Gabrielle d'Estrées, mistress of Henri IV; a portrait said to be of Mary, Queen of Scots, and one of her lover, Lord Darnley. Miniatures by Isaac Oliver depicted the Countess of Pembroke and Henry, Prince of Wales. Thomas Betts, John Hoskins, and the two Coopers were well represented, and in the eighteenth century Cosway alone was shown in some sixty miniatures and Plimer by thirty.

Glancing at two glorious Turners [Bishop Lawrence continues], one at each side of the large door, we passed into the next room, a perfect example of Louis XVI, walls, rugs, furniture, and ornaments of the richest of that day. Across the hall to the front, we entered the Fragonard Room, whose walls were drawn in by the builder to meet the exact dimensions and designs of the panels. [These are the Fragonards now in the Frick Collection.] In the center stood a table covered with a glass cabinet filled with beautiful jeweled boxes. A glimpse of the portrait of the most attractive boy that one has ever seen, probably by Velasquez, drew one into the Louis XV room, where there were beautiful cabinets and examples of Sèvres. Portraits of Queen Anne of Austria and her brother, Cardinal Ferdinand, by Rubens, looked down upon us.

As one went down the staircase, a shelf at the landing was filled with a number of china pug dogs, such as ladies collected in their parlors some thirty years ago. Mr. Morgan's devotion to his mother's memory retained these here, although from every other point of view they were out of harmony with the surroundings.

As we stepped down the last two or three stairs, Van Dyck's *Duke of Warwick* facing us directly, seemed to be walking toward us. Going from the hall to the two rooms at the back, we entered on the right the parlor where guests were received. Here great and graceful Gainsboroughs and Raeburns gave warmth to the atmosphere, while the furniture given by Louis XV to the King of Denmark seemed always to have belonged here. When, a few months before, Queen Alexandra and her sister, the Empress of Russia, were being shown about the house, one of them exclaimed, "Why, there are the chairs!" and the other said, "So they are." Mr. Morgan said, "What chairs?" "Why, our brother had those chairs but they disappeared and we never knew what had become of them; they must have been sold."

The vital center of the house was the adjoining room, Mr. Morgan's own. Over the mantel hung the portrait of his father; his portrait hung also over the mantel in his library in New York. On the right of the chimney hung the portrait of Miss Croker in her beautiful youth by Lawrence, and on the mantel beside it stood a large photograph of herself at the age of 93 given by her to Mr. Morgan. How many women would have the hardihood to encourage this contrast? One must say, however, that in the revelation of the growth of character, the contrast is in favor of the old lady. On the other side of the chimney hung Romney's portrait of Lady Hamilton reading the news of Nelson's victory, her eyes filled with glad surprise. Diagonally across from *Miss Croker* hung Sir Thomas Lawrence's full-length portrait of Miss Farren, Lady Derby. The walls were rich with other portraits and pictures, the tables and bookcases strewn with statuettes and works of art dating from 3000 B.C. up to the twentieth century, some of them left there by dealers for Mr. Morgan to inspect, others selected by himself in Rome, Egypt and elsewhere.

At a dinner party one evening, Mrs. Talbot, the wife of the then Bishop of Southwark, said to me, "What a mass of interesting things are in this house!" I answered, "Mrs. Talbot, the most interesting thing in this house is the host." For that reason, one thinks always of Mr. Morgan's chair in the corner near the fireplace, with *Miss Croker* overhead, the sun pouring in from the window and the song of a bullfinch, the most beautiful bird voice I ever heard, making the air rich with melody. Beside Mr. Morgan was always his card table, his pack of cards for solitaire at any moment and a box of great cigars nearby. Here he passed hours at a time, talking, thinking, dozing, and playing solitaire. Many smaller men make their room a keep from which all guests are excluded. Although his secretary passed the mornings in this room and dictation of telegrams might be going on, the doors were almost always open and we went in and out at will, sitting and talking,—indeed, that was the living-room downstairs for all the members of the party.

It was this atmosphere of domesticity in the midst of the richest of treasures that made Prince's Gate unique; everything in the house was a part of the house, and the house was the home of its master. To be sure, beneath were two large rooms of steel, each of them furnished with glass cases which were illuminated by electric lights. In the one was table china, rich and precious; in the other, great pieces of old silver for the center of the table. These were in the house not to be gazed upon by visitors but to be used every day.

Domestic as the house was, it was at the same time open to hundreds of visitors who had requested the privilege of Mr. Morgan and who presented his card. As one passed through the hall, he met two or three persons at a time, connoisseurs, artists, representatives of nobility from every country in Europe and from America, attended by the faithful Margaret, who, beginning as a young servant girl with his father, was the housekeeper,

[2 5]

guide and factotum of Prince's Gate. Henry, also a young servant of his father, was the butler who took up his story with the visitors when Margaret was overburdened.

The remarkable feature about this man of material wealth and splendor was that his personality mastered as well as pervaded it all. Every smallest ornament or richest picture had the hallmark of his individuality. And yet Mr. Morgan never talked of them or of the things that he owned except as he saw that they were of interest to others. His friends and the public unconsciously recognized this personality. Great as was his yacht, people never spoke of the *Corsair* and Mr. Morgan entering the harbor; it was Mr. Morgan on the *Corsair*. When he was away from his library, the library seemed empty. However rich the trappings, they took their proper place, merely as the trappings of the man. It was this that made his manner of life seem princely.

Mr. Morgan enjoyed London. It was the home of his father and the home of quite a fraction of his life. Business cares were there of course, as they were everywhere; nevertheless it was easier for him to break away from them there than in New York. His time was comparatively his own. His position in London too was unique. Recognized by everyone, but more independent of conventional and general social obligations than in New York, he was more at leisure to be the host, and where he had a small company of friends with whom he could talk in an unguarded way, he felt at ease. Two or three characteristics come to mind as I think of him in London. I doubt if any private citizen ever lived in as comfortable splendor as did Mr. Morgan. Some may have had more comfort, others more splendor, but his was splendor with comfort. It is a question open to debate as to whether he had a right to live in this way.

I never knew a man to whom in expenditure the question of dollars was of less interest nor one who so naturally surrounded himself with all that was richest, most convenient and artistic. He reached the climax of his abilities just as the financial world was flowing into great masses, and working in the midst of this, masses of wealth flowed towards him. They

[26]

came quickly and increasingly. His mind was intensely occupied with many things. He did not have time nor probably interest to enter into the philosophy of the use of wealth,—what proportion ought to be spent, what proportion to be given, or his obligations to the great mass of the people through some distribution of his property. Indeed, when one thinks of the short term of years in which Mr. Morgan lived in the way that I have described, one appreciates how natural it was for him to do very much as the rest of us do. When we have an increase of income, we naturally increase expenditure in various ways, private and public. We do not reason it out as to the exact proportion but in a rough way we try, taking things as they are, to do the right thing. Expenditure and wealth are all comparative, and while from a theoretical point of view Mr. Morgan might have given over his surplus income to somebody else to distribute, he did not himself have time to do it wisely. With a good conscience, he followed the traditions of his forbears and the habits of the best citizens. . . .

In the gathering of works of art, he doubtless took pleasure in acquisition. He liked to find the best and to know the best, and, given a man of his wealth, it is something to be grateful for that his fine taste prompted the selection of the finest. He well knew that practically every work of art that he bought was in time going back to the people. That the chief motive in the gathering of his collections was the love of acquisition, anyone who knew him would immediately deny. He had a love, almost a passion, for beautiful and interesting things for their own sake. As soon as the finest beauty and the real interest ceased, he dropped that subject, and it was on this account . . . that most of his collections were incomplete. Indeed, a remark which he dropped in Naples revealed, so it seemed to me, the principle which had guided him in the making of his collections.

Mrs. Burns [his sister] said to him the next day after our arrival, "Pierpont, aren't you going down to a certain dealer in Greek antiquities?" He answered, "No." "But," she said, "you have always gone there and bought and he has been courteous enough to send his car for your use." "No," he said, "I am not going there any more; I have done with Greek antiquities;

I am at the Egyptian." This together with the remark . . . , that when he had collected every piece of French porcelain of the finest that could be found outside of the museums, he stopped, makes me feel that there was a principle which guided him in the gathering of such a variety of collections.

His active mind also pressed him to move from interest to interest; hence we find in his collections the finest in miniatures, the best in English portraits and landscapes, the richest in Limoges and porcelains and bronzes, the best of Caxtons, the most interesting of manuscripts. . . . The persistency with which he would follow up what really interested him was remarkable. I remember his telling me how he obtained the Byron manuscripts. "I was told," he said, "in London, that the Byron manuscripts were in the possession of a lady, a relative of Byron, in Greece. Libraries in England were after them. I wanted them. I therefore, through the advice of an expert, engaged a man, gave him a letter of credit and told him to go to Greece and live [there] until he had gotten those manuscripts. Every once in a while, during several years, a volume would come which the relative had been willing to sell, until the whole was complete."

When Pierpont Morgan accepted the presidency of the Metropolitan Museum in 1904 it was abundantly clear that his imagination was inflamed by a grand design for the artistic enrichment of his native country. He had been elected a Patron of the Museum as early as 1871, and had served as a trustee continuously since 1888. He had also given a sum of money to build, as a memorial to his father, an art gallery adjacent to the Wadsworth Atheneum in Hartford, the city of his birth. Moreover the London houses could no longer contain the treasures which he was steadily amassing. Because of the tariff then existing on the importation of works of art into the United States, he did not feel that he could afford to bring them over until

Pierpont Morgan, by Frank Holl, 1888.

the statute had been changed. Many of the works of art accumulated after 1900 were therefore placed on loan at the Victoria and Albert Museum in South Kensington and the hopes of the English keepers were aroused. Had he not had such a clear vision of their ultimate destiny—which he was willing to entrust to his son, J. P. Morgan—it would have been much easier for him to leave his collections in London. It was true that many of his own and of his father's associations were English, but his belief in the destiny of America and his patriotism were convinced and deep-seated. He had, moreover, a brilliant example before his eyes. Sir Richard Wallace, who like him had spent long periods of his life away from his own country, had bequeathed his collections to remain intact at Hertford House as a museum for the nation. Pierpont Morgan resolved to create in New York a greater museum than anyone at that time dreamed it was possible to realize, and a library which would go down in history as comparing favorably to the Vatican, the Laurentian Library in Florence, and the most sumptuous assemblages of rare books in Paris, London, and Vienna.

His pleasure in purely personal luxury thus diminished as he raced against time, for he was already in his sixties, and he had yet to complete his life's work. We find him spending longer periods away from the business which was in the hands of his competent partners, and devoting himself to long cruises on the *Corsair,* and journeys on the Nile in his dahabiah, the *Khargeh.* Everywhere he went he was pursued by dealers who were on the way up and once proud aristocrats who were on the way down. His capacity for instant decision was a phenomenon scarcely seen since the time of Cardinal Mazarin. He was accused of not looking at the object when in reality he was looking into the eye of the man who was trying to sell it to him. That was, after all, how he had reached the summit in finance and it had paid off well. Those who counted on his reputed ignorance and lack of taste—a theory which was widespread among the "have-nots" of the trade—were badly fooled when the chips were down. Never in the history of collecting has anyone made his mistakes more shrewdly or more deliberately. As a mathematician he was sufficiently familiar with the law of averages to risk buying ready-made collections *en bloc*. And while it is fashionable among the fastidious to deprecate such wholesale connoisseurship, he chose his sources with care, and the fact remains that of the more than four thousand objects from his collections given to the Metropolitan Museum an informed guess would place the number now on permanent exhibition (and because of their quality likely to remain so) at something well over ninety per cent. An even higher percentage of excellence is true of the collections of the Library.

The energy with which the dealers sought to find Morgan's Achilles heel was little short of titanic. For several winters Canfield, "the perfect gambler," held a special class for the European art dealers who upon their arrival in New York thought it expedient to learn the card games to which Morgan was addicted. Any ruse to get by the secretary or the butler was considered fair game. A. S. Drey of Munich used to tell a story of how he finally established contact with him. The *New York Times* announced one morning that Mr. Morgan, who was about to leave for a Mediterranean cruise on the *Corsair,* had just completed negotiations for the purchase of the *Tornabuoni Princess* by Domenico Ghirlandaio. Drey thought very quickly and that same day caught the *Mauretania* for Cherbourg. He took the sleeper to Florence and went directly to the Grand Hotel where Morgan always stopped. Every day for three weeks he took his post from early morning to sundown in the refectory of the Ognissanti in front of Ghirlandaio's fresco of the *Last Supper*. Surely, he reasoned, a man who had paid such a princely sum for an example of this artist's work would make the pilgrimage to see his greatest masterpiece. Then one day Morgan, who was alone in Florence, walked into the room. In the relaxed manner of tourists before a great work of art the two men fell into casual conversation. The afternoon wore on and they returned together to the hotel for dinner. That evening they played cards and before he went to bed that night Drey claimed he had sold Morgan works of art running into six figures.

This may be apocryphal—merely a tall story for the trade—but it is significant for it shows the ability of this world financier to concentrate upon artistic detail. This quality comes out even more astonishingly in the long files of correspondence in the Library. The pattern of procedure was usually for Miss Greene to bring to his attention matters requiring a decision. The letters were placed in front of him and in his own hand he would write on them marginal comments and instructions, or he would tell Miss Greene orally what he wanted done. These letters, in French, German and Italian as well as in English, had clearly been read by him and had been fully understood. From these instructions Miss Greene would write the replies. Virtually never would Morgan write directly; he much preferred the telegraph or telephone, or a personal interview. He always had to see an object before he would decide whether to buy or reject it, and he liked to know the person he was buying it from. Like all collectors, he had his favorite advisers and dealers: Sir Hercules Read, William M. Laffan (proprietor of The New York *Sun*), Thomas B. Clarke, Bernard Quaritch, the Agnews, and Jacques Seligmann, to name only a few of the most trusted. Their letters are filled with a mutual respect for each other's taste and acumen, and give the lie to the deliberately distorted picture of Morgan painted by Roger Fry which appeared in Virginia Woolf's biography of 1940. But Fry was bitter because he had met his match; he had unfortunately found in Morgan what he least desired—a New Yorker who was sufficiently at home in England to recognize him for what he was, a second-class Englishman making a career of first-class American society.

From the turn of the century to the eve of the First World War the collections assembled primarily during the reign of Napoleon III fell one by one into Morgan's lap. In 1902 he purchased the Garland Collection of oriental porcelains which he discovered, after paying $100,000 for it, was not "complete." Thereupon he said to Henry Duveen, who had been the agent, "I shall be glad if you will complete it for me." That same year he purchased the celebrated Mazarin tapestry, now in Washington in the Widener Collection, for $350,000. There were rumors that it would be hung in the Abbey for the coronation of Edward VII, who had long been a friend of Morgan's, but in the end it was placed on loan in the South Kensington Museum. During the summer Morgan visited Germany, where he received the Kaiser aboard the *Corsair* at Kiel, and spent much time in the Berlin Museum with Dr. Bode. Not long afterwards he presented to the Kaiser a celebrated letter of Martin Luther to the Emperor Charles V because he thought it should properly remain in Germany. Italy also benefited from his generosity; in 1904 alone he gave $100,000 to help establish the American Academy in Rome, and he returned the Ascoli cope—one of the greatest examples of *opus Anglicanum* embroidery—to the Italian Government, although he had paid a dealer a rumored $15,000 for it in good faith, without knowing that it had been stolen during repairs to the Cathedral at Ascoli. On a later trip to Italy he paid a special call on the Minister of Education to assure him (which was scarcely necessary) that the Cattaneo Van Dycks had not entered the Morgan collection, after they had allegedly been smuggled out of Italy by a French dealer in the false bottom of a motor car. Three of these ultimately joined the Widener Collection and two, the Frick.

[3 2]

The years 1906 and 1907 were filled with opportunity. He purchased from Agnew's the Frans Hals portraits of Heer and Vrouw Bodolphe (now in the Stephen C. Clark Collection) together with some architectural fragments from the Basilica Ulpia in Trajan's Forum which he presented to the Metropolitan. The incomparable series of Roman frescoes from Boscoreale, a suburb of Pompeii, had already come to the Metropolitan through his generosity, as had the Raphael *Madonna* altarpiece which had been successively treasured by the Colonna family of Rome and the Kings of Naples. Finally at about this same time, after many months of negotiation, the Hoentschel Collection was acquired for 4,000,000 francs. This noted collection of *boiseries* and decorative elements of all kinds was in two parts. The decorative arts of the seventeenth and eighteenth centuries he gave to the Metropolitan Museum at this time; the Gothic sections, equally rich and varied, were to come in 1916 as the gift of his son.

The range and catholicity of these assemblages from all periods and civilizations are staggering to the imagination. Ancient art in its most disparate styles and techniques from 3000 B.C. to the fifth century A.D., including six large alabaster Assyrian reliefs from the palace of Ashur-nasir-pal at Nimrod; an assortment running into the hundreds of minor antiquities, seals and jewels from Egypt, Greece and the Aegean lands; sculpture of the Eighteenth Dynasty, and the Gréau Collection of ancient glass numbering over eight hundred items; silver dishes from Cyprus and the golden bowls of the Alban treasure; two collections of Gallo-Roman, Germanic, and Merovingian art consisting of personal ornaments of the barbaric tribes from the fall of the Roman Empire to the time of Charlemagne—the one gathered throughout France by Stanislas Baron, and the other assembled from excavations made by the German antiquary Queckenberg at Niederbreisig between Coblenz and Bonn.

These artifacts alone would bring any museum to the front rank but, taken in conjunction with the incredible sequences of hundreds of Byzantine and Romanesque objects for devotional use and domestic ornament, they suddenly placed the Metropolitan, when they were ultimately received, on a footing with the Cluny and the Victoria and Albert museums. To these were added specialized groups of comparable importance: Renaissance jewels and ornaments from every country; the Le Breton Collection of faïence from Rouen, Moustiers, Marseilles, and other French centers; the Marfels Collection of watches; and the Gutmann Collection of antique plate and bronzes of German Renaissance and Baroque workmanship. These are but a few of the various lots which were swept into the tidal wave of Morgan's enthusiasm.

The courage of the man was no less formidable than his appetite. In June, 1907, he agreed to buy from Duveen eleven paintings and five art objects from the Rodolphe Kann Collection, at a total cost of some $1,275,000. In accordance with his invariable custom, payment was deferred until the following year. The October panic, which Morgan stopped by demanding concerted action at meetings of financiers held in his new Library, could hardly have left him enthusiastic about such a future expenditure. But his word had been pledged, his confidence in his country was unshaken, and he proceeded with the purchase, acquiring among the paintings the superb *Annunciation* by Rogier van der Weyden, and the three Memlings now in the Morgan Library. His activity never slackened, and early in 1910 the memorial gallery in Hartford was completed and endowed.

During the next two years Pierpont Morgan became increasingly concerned that though he was endowed with many gifts, immortality was not one of them. Fear of newly enacted death duties in England emphasized the desirability of closing out Prince's Gate and transferring the collection to America. The air was filled with rumors that equally confiscatory legislation was to be introduced in the Con-

Portrait of a Man With a Pink, by Hans Memling, about 1470.
From the Rodolphe Kann Collection.

gress of the United States. He was in effect caught between the two stones of a seemingly inexorable mill. Meanwhile, a bill was passed by Congress permitting works of art and articles of manufacture over one hundred years old to enter the country duty free, and Morgan determined to transfer his collections to his native land as soon as practicable. Preoccupation with the problems of this mammoth moving operation did not prevent his going ahead with his program of acquisition. He bought the Knole tapestries from Lady Sackville and, for the Library, the Fairfax Murray Collection of drawings and a number of manuscripts of first importance. He was caught in a current which he was happy not to resist; even in that last cruise to Egypt and to Italy he was constantly being importuned by hopeful vendors. The correspondent of the London *Daily Mail* a week before the end sent back the following dispatch:

The Grand Hotel, where J. Pierpont Morgan is staying, may be compared to a closely besieged fortress. There is not an art dealer or antiquary in Rome who is not making desperate efforts to approach the banker with the offer of some 'extraordinary bargain.'

All sorts of odds and ends, valueless old pictures, china, lace and the like are unearthed from drawers, etc. by private persons who fondly believe they can call on Mr. Morgan, dispose of their goods and return home with bundles of bank notes. Waves of these amateur art dealers, most of whom carry mysterious bundles, sweep upon the hotel from early morning to late at night and are repulsed with the regularity of surf on the beach.

Hundreds of letters, the majority containing photographs and pictures of statues, arrive by every post from all parts of Italy. These are dealt with by a special staff of secretaries who, after glancing at the opening lines, throw them into a huge wastepaper basket. I saw 500 letters destroyed this morning.

When the news was finally cabled to the world that he had died there was endless speculation regarding the ultimate disposition of the Morgan collections. The *Times* of London made an estimate of their value at $60,000,000. The will left all works of art to J. P. Morgan, who knew his father's intentions (reaffirmed in the will) but was free to do with them as he saw fit. A great exhibition was held at the Metropolitan of substantially the whole of the vast art collection late in 1913 and early in 1914. The insurance valuation placed on what was exhibited was $28,000,000. Allowing for the value of the contents of the Library, and the objects that were retained by members of the family, the *Times* figure would not seem to be unduly exaggerated. It was not until 1918, when the estate had been somewhat clarified, that the share of the collection which the Museum was to receive as a gift was finally determined. It had unfortunately been necessary to sell a large number of the very finest pieces in order to meet taxes and maintain the liquidity of this very large estate.

A special wing was provided by the city to house the collections the Museum was to receive, and it was a stipulation of the gift that the Morgan objects be kept together in the Morgan Wing for fifty years. In 1943, just a few weeks before his own death, the son and heir, J. P. Morgan, sent for the director of the Museum and said with characteristic generosity and vision, "I am in complete sympathy with your plans for revamping the collections of the Museum and for presenting them in a more logical fashion. The stipulation which I made many years ago would prevent your accomplishing this end. I do not wish to stand in your way." And he handed the director a formal letter addressed to the Board of Trustees releasing them from the restriction.

Today the Morgan collections are distributed throughout the Metropolitan Museum. Other segments are at Hartford and with very few exceptions the objects which the estate was obliged to sell have found their way to public institutions in the United States. Only the Pierpont Morgan Library remains virtually intact as a memorial to its founder.

When the Library was completed over sixty years ago it was one of the Seven Wonders of the Edwardian World. Charles Follen McKim, who had already in a number of buildings—particularly the Seth Low Pantheon for Columbia University on Morningside Heights—proclaimed his passion for the classical tradition, had encompassed in this small white marble pavilion, so redolent of the Palazzo del Te in Mantua, the whole of his equally gay affinity for the Renaissance of Italy. The lavish enthusiasm of his patron had made possible the employment of a group of sensitive collaborators, the sculptors Edward Clark Potter and Andrew O'Connor, and the painter Harry Siddons Mowbray. The latter, born in Alexandria of English parents, had shown his mettle in the decorations for the University Club. He was a pupil of Bonnat but his sojourns in Italy had endowed him with a sense of neo-classic measure and refinement not known since the Age of Adam in England and of Bulfinch in this country. The great Renaissance-style bronze doors imported from Italy made a stately entrance to Mowbray's authoritarian decorations for the central rotunda, whose severe and classical atmosphere imposed restraint on the spacious "double-cube" room to the East and the Morgan "study" to the West of it. Tapestries, bronzes, and a superb selection of antiquities and art objects of the first fifteen centuries of the Christian era were here assembled with that rare and paradoxical blend of magnificence and simplicity which saves this jeweled casket, nestling down as it does between the towers and

[3 7]

hanging gardens of a modern Babylon, from being merely a human-istic witticism, and makes it instead one of the loveliest things ever done on this side of the Atlantic.

To enumerate the treasures of this Library would go far beyond the limits of this notice on the founder. In manuscripts of the Middle Ages and the Renaissance alone it now houses, in the words of Seymour de Ricci's *Census,* "the most extensive and the most beauti-fully selected series of manuscripts existing on the American Con-tinent, and it may truthfully claim to be superior in general quality to all but three or four of the greatest national libraries of the Old World." Between his father's death in 1913 and his own in 1943, J. P. Morgan added to the original nucleus many of the Library's most precious books and manuscripts. In 1924, by his munificent gift and by a special act of the Legislature of New York State, the building and its contents became a public reference library. From that time to the present, under the guidance of Miss Greene, Frederick B. Adams, Jr., and now of Charles Ryskamp and their distinguished collaborators, the founder's tradition has been maintained in steady growth of the Library, directed by a Board of Trustees which num-bers sixteen members under the presidency of Henry S. Morgan.

The present contents therefore must be considered in their en-tirety as a collaborative enterprise of collecting extending over a period of more than seventy-five years. To name but a handful of the illuminated manuscripts, one must inevitably include the ninth-century Lindau Gospels with its jeweled Carolingian cover, the eleventh-century Gospels of Matilda, Countess of Tuscany, the tenth-century Spanish Commentary of Beatus on the Apocalypse, and the fifteenth-century Dutch Hours of Catherine of Cleves. One must likewise mention in the same breath the ancient papyri, Dioscorides' *De materia medica* in Greek, and incomparable illustrated manuscripts from Armenia, Persia, and Egypt. Then too there are other princely

Jeweled Cover of the Lindau Gospels.

manuscripts of Western Europe on secular themes: historical chronicles, romances of chivalry, collections of poetry, treatises on hunting, and scientific works.

The autograph letters and modern literary manuscripts comprise one of the largest sections of these collections now reaching high into the tens of thousands of items. The early printed books include the great rarities of the Renaissance presses of Europe and the British Isles. Among the bookbindings all the famous masters and collectors of every period up to 1800 are included. The cabinet of drawings—the core of which is the Fairfax Murray Collection acquired in 1910—is the most important in the United States.

One achievement of Pierpont Morgan the collector has been best expressed in the words of the already quoted editorial in *The Burlington Magazine* for May, 1913:

[His collecting] produced in the general public an altogether new reverence for ancient art. The Philistine, who had been accustomed to regard art as a trifling and frivolous embroidery upon life, began to realize that it might occupy a more important place in the scheme of things than he had ever supposed possible.

Pierpont Morgan was the greatest figure in the art world that America has yet produced, a visionary and a patron such as we never knew before, nor ever shall again.

When his will was published, it was easy to recognize in one significant passage the principle that had guided his purchasing:

I have been greatly interested for many years in gathering my collections . . . and it has been my desire and intention to make some suitable disposition of them . . . which would render them permanently available for the instruction and pleasure of the American people.

Never in the course of the history of collecting either in the United States or abroad has any private man—apart from reigning sovereigns —made so important or so generous a gift of art to the public.